# Nightmare in Europe

Judy S. Walter

Layout and Design by
Penny Maxson

*S/P*

Sluser Publishing

Printed in the USA

ISBN 978-0-578-10318-1

Cover photo taken at Dachau, Germany
by Kaitlyn Trait

*S/P*

Sluser Publishing
P.O. Box 6
Fayetteville, PA 17222

# Author's Note

You may wonder why I've written a book about the Holocaust. It happened so long ago - and I am not an historian. I did, however, teach the Holocaust in conjunction with The Diary of Anne Frank and Night. Why write a book?

Many Holocaust survivors moved to the United States. Many left Europe before the mass murders. In my lifetime, I have met a number of survivors. They all want to tell their stories. They want people to remember the victims who suffered and died at the hand of an evil dictator.

The fear of survivors is that as they age and die, eventually there will be no one left to tell their stories. The deaths of eleven million people will be forgotten. They fear that the racism and hatred that brought about the Holocaust will be allowed to resurface.

It is in their honor that I have written this book, so that the world will NEVER FORGET the nightmare that was the Holocaust.

*Judy S. Walter*

Virginia Holocaust Museum in Richmond, VA
Photo by Penny Maxson

# Table of Contents

# CHAPTER ONE

## Antisemitism

# Antisemitism

The word antisemitism refers to the hatred and discrimination toward the Jews simply because they are Jews. This discrimination did not start with Hitler, but actually goes all the way back to the crucifixion of Jesus and maybe even before that. Eventually the Jews became political targets in Europe. They were hated for their ideas, beliefs and even the jobs they held in life. They were resented throughout Europe.

Hitler capitalized on this hatred. He made it the mission of the Third Reich to wipe out all of the Jews in Europe. The hatred that began centuries ago culminated in the Holocaust.

Think about this for a moment. Are you responsible today for something your great-great-great-great grandfather did? The rational answer is no. So how could the twentieth century Jews of Europe be responsible for crucifying Christ? It just became an excuse to hate people.

Some of this hatred - antisemitism - persists today. In 2007, Jewish graves were vandalized in the Ukraine in Europe. Violent acts are still committed against the Jews worldwide even today.

How would you like to be spat upon, cursed, called names, or hit just because you are Jewish? Maybe you would have to move from your neighborhood because it is no longer safe for Jews to live there. Perhaps you would be banned from school. You could no longer see your doctor. The local hospital will not treat you. There are stores where you can no longer shop. You can't participate in sports because no Jews are allowed.

This is unfair treatment. This is racism. This is antisemitism.

# CHAPTER TWO

## Hitler Gains Control
## of Germany

After World War I, Germany had to pay money to the other countries for the damage caused during the war. In the treaty that ended the war, there were 414 clauses directed against Germany. Chaos reigned after the war. The German people felt total defeat. They had lost their national honor.

Economic times were bad all over the industrialized world, including Germany. As the 1920s headed toward the stock market crash, factories in Germany closed. People were out of work. There was not enough food or money to go around.

Austrian born Adolf Hitler, an army corporal, took advantage of this situation. A great speaker, he was able to take over his political party (National Socialist) and eventually become the leader of Germany. He promised that people would have jobs and food. He also promised to make Germany a great country again and to restore Germany's honor. He also wanted to create a pure race - an Aryan race.

When the German leaders installed Hitler as Chancellor in 1933, twenty million people tuned in on the radio to hear him speak. He declared that the destiny of Germany was in his hands.

When Hitler became dictator of Germany in 1933, he and his men set about to imprison and destroy anyone who did not agree with him. Newspaper editors who spoke out against him became easy targets. Hitler and the Nazis took away individual freedoms. Laws were changed. Other political parties were not allowed - only the Nazi Party (National Socialist).

Hitler was a great speaker. He would stand before crowds - in a car, on a platform, or on a balcony - and give excited speeches promising jobs and prosperity for the German people. He also talked about the Germans being the "Master Race." He said that the other races were inferior, especially the Jews.

The Jews were decent people. They were doctors, dentists, lawyers, scientists, teachers, jewelers, bankers, shop keepers, and farmers. They were productive members of society. Their ONLY crime was that they were Jewish.

Hitler did not like anyone who was different from what he believed his master race should be.

He and the Nazis practiced discrimination against many groups: Jews, Poles (Polish People), Russians, gypsies, Jehovah's Witnesses, the disabled, and anyone else who was considered inferior.

Hitler also did not like intellectuals (the thinking group). They were a real threat to him. He wanted the masses to follow him blindly, without thinking. Intellectuals thought for themselves and tried to get others to see how destructive Hitler was. They had to be rounded up, sent to concentration camps, and killed.

Hitler had his army march into towns, villages, and cities all over Europe. There was no place safe in Europe while Hitler and the Nazis were in power. Hitler is an example of how one man can change the world. In his case, it was for evil.

# CHAPTER THREE

Propaganda and
Youth Camps

# Propaganda

Hitler used propaganda to sway the German people against the Jews. The Nazis published a weekly newspaper which said, "The Jews are our misfortune." The newspaper also ran cartoons which made the Jews look less than human. By 1938, the newspaper had a distribution of half a million copies weekly. Unfortunately - then and now - people tend to believe what they read in newspapers.

This was an effective tool in turning many people against the Jews. It's no wonder the Nazis rounded up editors of newspapers that spoke out against Hitler.

Add to the Nazi newspaper Hitler's rousing speeches to the crowds. The result was the brainwashing of the German people.

Daily, the German public and school children were brainwashed into believing that Jews were the cause of all evil in society. They were portrayed as subhuman. To disagree was to commit treason against Germany.

# Youth Camps

Another method Hitler used to brainwash the German people was the establishment of youth camps. By 1936 all children aged ten were required to join the Hitler Youth. These camps trained children and teens to be loyal to Hitler and Nazism. Children were instructed to keep their eyes and ears open and report anyone who said or did anything against the Nazi Party.

Children's loyalty was first of all to Hitler. He came before their parents.

Hitler was very smart. He realized that if the youth could be persuaded to believe in him and the Nazi Party, they would be loyal followers who would always do his bidding. Young people can be a powerful force. As they grew up, they would become part of his army. There would be no stopping Hitler, or so he thought.

# CHAPTER FOUR

## Kristallnacht

## Kristallnacht

The literal translation of this word is night of crystal, but it became known as the night of the broken glass. November 9-10, 1938, saw a wave of violence and destruction perpetrated by Hitler Youth and Nazi SS (Storm Troopers) against the Jews. They targeted Jewish owned businesses, hospitals, and synagogues, as well as Jewish homes. This destruction took place in Germany, Austria, and the part of Czechoslovakia known as the Sudetenland.

The instructions for these riots came from high ranking Nazi officials. The rioters shattered windows and destroyed over 1,000 synagogues. Many were set on fire. Many homes and businesses were also burned. Approximately 7,500 Jewish owned businesses were vandalized.

Close to 100 Jews were murdered. Another 30,000 were arrested. It was a night of unprecedented terror and destruction.

Laws were passed aimed at removing the Jews from public life and society in general. Some laws categorized people as Jewish if they had a Jewish grandparent. Signs went up everywhere saying that Jews were unwelcome.

After Kristallnacht, Jews were not allowed in universities, theatres, and many other places. Jewish lawyers could not practice law. Jewish doctors were not allowed to treat non-Jewish patients.

By 1939, all Jews had to carry identification cards that said they were Jewish. After the Germans invaded Poland in 1939, they ordered all Jews in occupied countries to wear the yellow star. In 1941, the Nazis provided the yellow star with the word Jude to all Jews in Germany. This made it easy for the Germans to recognize the Jews. This was part of their plan to separate the Jews from the rest of society. It was a terrible time to be living in Europe.

In 1933 there were more than nine million Jews in Europe. By the end of World War II, there were only about three million left. Hitler and the Nazis had almost succeeded in ridding Europe of the Jews. In some cases, entire villages and towns were totally wiped out.

Forbidden for Jews.   Photo by Penny Maxson

# CHAPTER FIVE

## Ghettos

# Ghettos

The establishment of ghettos was a phase in Hitler's plan to murder all of the Jews of Europe. All together, there were about 1,000 ghettos during this time. The Germans would round up all of the Jews in a city and force them into a confined area in another part of the city.

The two largest ghettos were the Warsaw Ghetto and the Lodz Ghetto. In the case of the Warsaw Ghetto, over 400,000 Jews were housed in the center of the city. Most ghettos were enclosed with brick walls or barbed wire fences.

There was never enough food - never enough heat in the winter. Often there was no heat, no running water. People starved. They came down with diseases. Life in the ghetto was horrible. The Jews also had to wear a yellow star (star of David) on the outside of their coats.

If they were caught outside the ghetto, they were usually shot. After a period of time, Jews living in ghettos were rounded up and transported to one of the concentration camps. Often it was a death camp where they were killed.

## Pets

Do you have a pet cat or dog? Imagine having to leave your beloved pet behind so that you and your family could escape or go into hiding. That's what so many people had to do.

Many Jews all over Europe had to leave their animals behind while they escaped to another country or went into hiding. Anne Frank, a twelve year old Jewish girl who has become known around the world after death because she wrote a daily diary while she and others were in hiding in Holland, had a cat that she had to leave behind. That had to break her heart.

Although Anne Frank's story is well known, it is just one of hundreds of stories of life in hiding during the Holocaust.

Here's another thought: people were given ration cards to get food. There were no ration cards for dog or cat food.

# CHAPTER SIX

## Concentration Camps

# Concentration Camps

Listed below are just a few of the 1,000 concentration camps in Europe between 1933 and 1945. Some camps were labor camps that assisted in the war effort. Others were death camps, responsible for the murder of over six million Jews and over five million non-Jews.

Sobibor - Poland
Auschwitz - Birkenau - Poland
Ravensbruck - Germany
Dachau - Germany
Bergen - Belsen - Germany
Buchenwald - Poland
Treblinka - Poland
Krakow - Poland
Flossenburg - Germany
Mauthausen - Austria
Theresienstadt - Czechoslovakia

# Dachau

During WWI, Dachau was a munitions factory. In 1933, it was turned into the first concentration camp to house political prisoners and Communist party officials. Theodore Eicke designed the layout of the camp and established the rules. In 1934 Eicke became an Inspector General over all concentration camps. Dachau became the first camp to experience the mass murder of innocent people.

Anyone who disagreed with the Nazi Party became a political opponent, subject to imprisonment. Today in the U.S. we take freedom of speech for granted. We can freely disagree with political leaders. That was not the case in Nazi Germany. To speak out against Hitler and the Nazi party was to write your own death warrant.

Dachau, by the way, is located in the beautiful state of Bavaria in Southern Germany. It's hard to believe that such a camp existed in such an otherwise beautiful area. I've been to Bavaria, but not to Dachau.

My former student, Kaitlyn Trait visited Dachau a couple of years ago. She told me that she could feel that she was standing on ground where innocent blood had been shed.

At Dachau and elsewhere, Jewish prisoners were treated worse than other prisoners. Inhumane medical experiments were conducted on prisoners at Dachau. When a prisoner became sick, he still had to work. Only after his temperature reached 104 degrees would he be sent to the camp doctor who did little to help.

Dachau was built to hold 5,000 prisoners but toward the end of the war held as many as 30,000. A barracks could comfortably sleep 200, but as time went on, held as many as 1,600. These were human beings just like you and me.

PHOTOS of DACHAU

All photos of
Dachau Concentration Camp
Memorial Site

Taken by Kaitlyn Trait

KZ-Gedenkstätte Dachau
Dachau Concentration Camp Memorial Site
"Dachau: die Bedeutung dieses Namens ist aus der Deutschen Geschichte nicht auszulöschen. Er steht für alle Konzentrationslager, die Nationalsozialisten in ihrem Herrschaftsbereich errichtet haben."
(Eugen Kogon)
"Dachau: the significance of this name will never be erased from German history. It stands for all concentration camps which the Nazis established in their territory."
(Eugen Kogon)

Where prisoners entered

Where prisoners slept

Toilets without privacy

Entrance to showers

Shower -- really gas chamber

Cremation ovens

Cremation ovens

Prisoners were shot standing over trenches.

Guard tower

Doors were locked.

A cleaned up Dachau

## Auschwitz

Auschwitz was established in Poland in 1940 by the Germans. It became the largest death camp during the Nazi rule. More than one million people were murdered in Auschwitz. They were mostly Jews.

Auschwitz was divided into Auschwitz I and Auschwitz-Birkenau. Above the gate into the camp hangs the sign: "Arbeit macht frei," meaning work will make you free. This was another Nazi lie. There was no freedom here - only slavery and death.

Originally the buildings at Auschwitz were used to house the Polish military. The Germans evicted the residents surrounding the camp. This made it easy for them to turn Auschwitz into a death camp where about 70,000 prisoners were murdered.

The second part of the camp, Auschwitz II-Birkenau was built as the main extermination camp. More than 960,000 Jews were killed here, as well as 19,000 gypsies and 75,000 Poles.

People were brought to Auschwitz, as well as

other concentration camps, by train. We are not talking about luxury trains. We are basically talking about cattle cars. The people were literally herded onto cattle train cars. Eighty to one hundred people filled each car.

You can see one of these train cars at the U.S. Holocaust Museum in Washington, D.C., and at the Virginia Holocaust Museum in Richmond, VA.

The word "Holocaust" has Greek origin. The definition is "sacrifice by fire." People entering Auschwitz could see the flames and smoke coming from the chimneys of the crematories. They could smell the burning flesh. Ashes from the burned bodies fell from the sky just like falling snow.

The camp - Auschwitz - still exists today as a memorial. It is a state museum and it is open to the public to tour. A former teacher at the high school where I taught visited Auschwitz. She spoke about it at lunch one day. The horrible reality of Auschwitz cannot be denied.

As I sit here today in front of the window writing and watching large snow flakes fall, I am reminded of the scenes I've read about where

Jewish people entering Auschwitz by train saw ashes descending from the chimneys of the crematories like falling snow. I am so glad I was born after the war and in America. Those are two things over which I had no control - time and place of birth. No one does.

## Sobibor

Sobibor was a death camp in eastern Poland. Every day trains would bring prisoners to the camp. They were told it was a work camp. The Nazis lied to them.

The prisoners had to leave their suitcases on the ground. They were then divided into two lines. The women and children were in one line. The men and older boys were in the other line. The officer in charge would ask for professional workers - shoemakers, seamstresses, etc. They would get out of the line and be taken to where they would work. All other prisoners were taken to the showers; however, the showers were really gas chambers where they were all gassed to death.

There were 600 prisoners housed at Sobibor. At one point, several Jewish leaders and Jewish Russian soldiers organized a revolt. They killed many of the German leaders and guards. Over 300 prisoners escaped from Sobibor. Afterwards the Germans closed the camp.

# CHAPTER SEVEN

## Fritz Solmitz

## Fritz Solmitz

Remember I said that the Nazis rounded up newspaper editors? One such person was Fritz Solmitz. Let me tell you something about his background.

Solmitz was born into a wealthy Jewish family in Berlin in 1893. He was well educated, earned his doctorate in 1921, and worked as a lawyer and judge. Prior to that, however, WWI interrupted his studies. He saw horrible suffering and death during the war. This caused him to become a pacifist - someone who is against war and violence,

For three years, Solmitz was in charge of the Department of Public Welfare in Berlin. Then he moved to Luebeck and became the editor of a Social Democratic newspaper called Leubecker People's Messenger. He even mentored the young Willie Brandt.

Solmitz watched Hitler's rise to power and knew that his intentions were not good, to say the least. Solmitz tried to warn the German people through his newspaper writings. He spoke out against Hitler. As a result, when Hitler came to power in 1933, Solmitz, along with other opposition leaders, was arrested and tortured in Fuhlsbeuttel Prison. The Nazis had turned Fuhlsbeuttel Prison into a concentration camp to incarcerate and torture political prisoners. It became known as a place of suffering, torture and death.

Solmitz wrote about his treatment in prison on cigarette papers and hid them in his pocket watch. This was before the Nazis started confiscating personal possessions. After his death, his pocket watch along with his other belongings were given to his wife, Karoline. He had also instructed her to take the children and flee Germany as soon as possible. It would be five years until she was able to accomplish this.

In 1938, the Nazis established Neuengamme Concentration Camp outside Hamburg. Fuhlsbeuttel is considered a branch of Neuengamme. Today, the pocket watch and writings of Fritz Solmitz are on display there, having been donated by his daughter.

Mrs. Solmitz lost her husband to Nazi brutality.

His children lost their father. His grandchildren lost an opportunity to know their grandfather.

You may wonder if all this is true. I was acquainted with the son of Fritz Solmitz. I also had the privilege of working in the same school with the grand-daughter of Fritz Solmitz. In fact, she spoke to my classes when I taught the Holocaust unit. I count her among my friends.

# CHAPTER EIGHT

## Rescuers

## Corrie Ten Boom

I met Corrie Ten Boom years ago, during her visit to the U.S. after the publication of her book, The Hiding Place. Corrie and her family were not Jewish. They were Dutch Christians.

The Ten Booms were very devout Christians. Corrie worked with a group of learning disabled children. She taught them about Jesus, the Bible, and faith. She read stories from the Bible to them. When the Germans invaded her town in Holland, they made her stop teaching the children. They had no use for people who were learning challenged.

Mr. Ten Boom was a famous watch maker in Holland. His daughter Corrie became the first licensed woman watch maker in Holland. Their home and shop were in the same building, which was typical in Europe at that time.

During Hitler's round up of the Jews in Europe, Corrie and her family built a secret hiding place in their home and took in Jews. Eventually the Nazis found out about the activities of the Ten Boom family and arrested them. Corrie and her sister were taken to Ravensbruck in Germany. Her father was also imprisoned.

Her faith, her belief in God kept Corrie going while she was in Ravensbruck. She had even been able to smuggle a Bible into the concentration camp. Corrie talked to the other women prisoners about God. The only time her faith wavered was when she witnessed a German guard beating her sister.

Physically, Corrie was a stronger woman than her frail sister. Her sister's health deteriorated while they were in prison. Both her sister and her father died while in the concentration camps. Corrie was released because of an error in paperwork. The next day all women her age were put to death - murdered.

The Friesen Clock which hung on the wall in the Ten Boom home and had been in the family for over 150 years, now is on display in the Virginia Holocaust Museum. You can read about the Ten Boom family's efforts to save the Jews and their ultimate capture and imprisonment in Corrie's book, The Hiding Place. It also recounts the daily atrocities she and her sister Betsy suffered while at Ravensbruck.

# Irene Sendler

There were many people who risked their lives during Hitler's reign to save the Jewish people. One such person was a social worker named Irene Sendler. She was born into a Catholic family in Warsaw, Poland, in 1910.

Her father, a doctor, died in 1917. Leaders in the Jewish community offered to pay for her education. Perhaps that was the beginning of her ties to the Jews.

One of the things Sendler did was make false documents for Jewish families. She also joined a resistance group in Warsaw to aid the Jews. This was a very dangerous thing to do because the Germans killed Polish families who hid Jews. In other countries, they arrested them and sent them to concentration camps.

Because Sendler worked for the Social Welfare Department, she was given a permit to enter the Warsaw Ghetto. The Germans wanted her to look for typhus which they did not want to spread outside the Ghetto. This gave her the opportunity to smuggle Jewish children out of the Ghetto.

She and her helpers used ambulances and other methods to get them out.

Polish families and Catholic orphanages took the children. The names of the children were placed in jars and buried. They were given new, non-Jewish names.

In 1943, the Germans arrested Sendler and tortured and planned to execute her. The Zegota (organization to aid the Jews) bribed the guards and got her released. She was, however, listed among those executed. She stayed in hiding until the war was over.

Irene Sendler was honored many times after the war for her work in saving 2,500 Jewish children. She died in Warsaw in 2008.

## Gertrude Babilinska

Imagine that you are a middle aged single woman working in a wealthy Jewish home. One day because the Nazis have taken over your town in Poland, the child's mother asks you to wear her wedding band and take the child and escape. You are asked to raise him as your own son rather than the son of Jewish parents.

That is exactly what Gertrude was asked to do. Gertrude, a Catholic, risked her life to save a Jewish child. She had to move from town to town. There were times when she and Michael (the Jewish boy) narrowly escaped the Nazis.

At the end of the war, they ended up in a DP camp (displaced persons) in Germany. Eventually, she and Michael got on a ship that was bound for Israel, the Jewish homeland. It was a long and perilous trip. They were even attacked at sea, but they finally made it to Israel.

Gertrude spent the rest of her life in Israel. She died in 1995 at the age of 93. Michael now lives in New York. His father was gassed to death at Auschwitz. His mother had become sick and died shortly after escaping the Nazis in Warsaw.

## Stefania Podgorska

Stefania was born in 1925 in Poland. Her parents were Catholic farmers. Her father died from illness in 1938. Stefania went into the nearby city to find work in order to help support her family. This is how she came to live with a Jewish family in the city. They were good to her and treated her just like a family member.

In 1941 the Germans took over the city. Stefania's Jewish family was sent to the ghetto. Her own mother was sent to Germany to work in a labor camp, leaving Helena (Stefania's younger sister) to be cared for by her sister.

Before the Jewish family left for the ghetto, they gave their house to Stefania. Instead of thinking only of themselves, the teenage Stefania and her sister rescued Jews who were able to escape from the ghetto. One is the son of her Jewish family. His parents are later deported and killed.

Stefania hides thirteen Jews in the attic of the house until the Nazis force her to leave. She then finds another house where she and her sister can live and keep the Jews in hiding until the Russian liberation of the city. For over two years, the teenage Stefania risked her life to work and get food and clothing for them and keep the Jews hidden from the Germans.

After the war Stefania married one of the Jews she rescued. Eventually they moved to the United States.

# CHAPTER NINE

Regina Fields, Survivor

Regina in Poland with her younger sister

Regina in 2012, living in the U.S.

## Regina Fields

Regina was born in Stanislawow, Poland in 1923. The town was located in Eastern Poland near the Russian border. By 1931, out of a population of over 72,000, the Jews numbered around 25,000. By the end of WWII, only 1,500 Jews had survived. The Germans had almost totally annihilated the Jewish population.

As respected members of the community, life was good for Regina and her family until the war. Her parents owned a dry goods store. However, from 1939 - 1941, their town came under Russian control. The Russians even confiscated the family's dry goods store. However, Regina's family was still able to live in their home, although a Russian judge came to live with them. It was the custom of the occupying government to assign people to live among the townspeople.

Then things changed drastically. In 1941, the Nazis (Germans) took over Stanislawow. The Jews had to surrender all their valuable possessions. Regina's parents and other neighbors got together and put their valuables - such as silver candlesticks, silver cups,etc. - into a large kettle. They buried this in the ground under a shed in Regina's back yard. A sliver chalice was one of the hidden possessions. Regina's grandfather's name was inscribed on it. Regina was able to retrieve it. This chalice was later used by her children at their weddings and on other religious occasions.

After the Nazis arrived, one of the first things they did was round up and kill about 500 Jewish doctors, lawyers, teachers, and other professional men. Then came the big massacre in October. According to Regina, when the Germans knocked on the door and ordered the Jews out, they did not know what was happening. In their innocence, they followed the Germans, perhaps thinking they were being taken to work. In reality they were being escorted to their death.

About 8,000 to 12,000 Jews were rounded up and taken to a cemetery which was surrounded by an iron fence. The Germans allowed some to return home to collect their valuable possessions. The remainder were shot to death over open graves and a trench. Because Regina and her family were late arriving at the cemetery, they missed the mass execution.

Next the Germans established a Jewish Ghetto on the poor side of town. All remaining Jews had to move there. German soldiers came into the Ghetto daily and shot people - for no reason.

Regina and the other young people were taken out of the Ghetto to work at a chicken plant. Regina suffered scars on her legs from carrying buckets of lime that spilled onto her. The lime was used to preserve chicken eggs.

There was a family named Bashuk that lived outside the Ghetto who was familiar with Regina's family's store. When Regina would leave the Ghetto for work, she would smuggle family possessions and take them to Mrs. Bashuk in exchange for food for her family. Many people in the Ghetto were dying from starvation and disease.

One day Regina's father did not return from work. Regina's mother said someone had to survive and it would be Regina. Her mother encouraged her to escape and seek a hiding place in the Bashuk home. A young man at the plant was planning to escape also. He, too, was friends with Mrs. Bashuk and had even made a door to the entrance of Mrs. Bashuk's attic.

The young man and Regina were caught talking at work. The guard struck Regina in the face with a whip. This incident was the catalyst to make Regina decide it was time to leave and go into hiding. Instead of going home to the Ghetto, Regina escaped and hid in Mrs. Bashuk's attic. The young man and another woman escaped also before the Germans killed the Jews in the Ghetto, including Regina's mother and her sister.

Some of Regina's cousins also survived. They were hidden in the home of a Ukrainian family under the floor boards where they had to sit on a bench.

While living in the attic, Regina had many close calls, but remained safe until the Russians liberated her town. Afterward Regina met and eventually fell in love with one of the Russian officers, also a Jew. He had to return to Russia to demobilize and say good-bye to his family, but within a year he left his homeland to join Regina. They were married in a displaced persons camp in Bavaria, Germany. Eventually they came by boat to the U.S. The year was 1950.

After coming to the U.S., Regina could not write or call Mrs. Bashuk. If anyone would have found out that she had hidden the Jews, she and her family would have suffered. Instead of being treated like heroes in Poland, they would have been outcasts. The Poles did not like Jews, and Hitler hated both Poles and Jews.

Regina's husband was a graduate of Moscow University. Before WWII, he was a lecturer. When they came to America, he became a college professor. Regina taught nursery school for thirty-nine years at a Jewish run nursery school. She was loved by the children and their parents.

Today, at age 89, Regina is a very proud mother, grandmother, and great-grandmother. She was the only one in her immediate family to survive the Holocaust, and she is thankful to God for having blessed her.

It was an honor and a pleasure for me to meet and talk with Regina and listen to her story.

# CHAPTER TEN

Helena O'Hare, Survivor

## Helena O'Hare

For Helena, life changed drastically in 1943 when she was thirteen years old. She lived in the part of Poland which is now the Ukraine. She, her two brothers, and their mother (a widow) lived in the same house as her grandparents. The grandparents lived in the main part of the house and had large furniture blocking the doorway to Helena's part. The house was in a wooded area.

Helena's cousin Maria lived nearby. Early one morning in June - about 4 AM - they went to pick berries. While they were gone, the Germans came assisted by the Polish men they had recruited. They would go in and pull people out of their houses and then burn down the houses. They took Helena's grandparents out. Her mother took the two boys and hid under the mattress.

One of the Polish men was a friend. He stood in front of the door that was covered by furniture and was the entrance to Helena's apartment. The Germans left without torching their house.

Helena and Maria could hear noise and shouting, so they went back to find out what was going on. At that point the Germans had put people into three lines. They shoved Maria and Helena into lines. One line was old people. Another was young people who were strong enough to work in Germany. The last line was people who would be sent back, including her mother.

Helena being a thin and frail child, was in the death line. Maria was in the work line. Helena begged a German soldier to let her go with her cousin to work. Finally, the soldier grabbed Helena's grandmother and put her in the death line in Helena's place. She watched as they shot her grandmother to death.

Helena and Maria, along with others, were put on a train car - cattle car - to be transported to Germany to work. They were in the car for three to five days with no food or water. Finally, the train stopped. The Germans took the people off and told them to drink from a mud puddle. Helena played on the fatherly instincts of one of the soldiers until he allowed her to drink from his canteen. He also gave her a piece of chocolate.

Helena was separated from her cousin and

sent to live with a German couple and work on their farm. They treated her well. The family had sons in the war. They felt if they were good to Helena, God would return their sons safely to them. That is what happened.

While living with the family, Helena would steal food and take into the city to her cousin. She eventually confessed to the farmer's wife, and she forgave Helena.

The war ended when Helena was sixteen. She was put in a Polish DP (displaced persons) camp. There was no food. She and a friend walked to the American Zone in the middle of the night. At this point Helena had a lung disease and was hospitalized. A nurse got penicillin and gave it to Helena. This saved her life.

Helena was moved to another camp. There she signed up to go to school in Berlin, where she learned shorthand and typing. She then had to go back to camp and work.

In 1947, she signed up to work abroad. A Canadian man took her to a ship bound for Canada. She landed in Nova Scotia. She was then taken to Toronto and later to Hamilton, Ontario.

Because of her skills, she was given a job working in an office at a cotton mill. Eventually she realized that workers in the mill were making more money than she was, so she left the office and went to work in the mill.

It was there that she met the man who would become her husband. They had five children. Helena is still living today and is in her eighties. I spoke with a close family friend who gave me Helena's story with her permission. I submitted questions which Helena answered.

# CHAPTER ELEVEN

## Racism

# Racism

Racism involves disliking or even hating people because of their skin color or where they were born. It is judging and disliking people for something over which they have no control. Let me give you an example of what I mean.

I don't know about you, but when I was born, there was no one standing there with a color palette asking me what color I would like to be. Had there been, I might have chosen red or blue or turquoise. Wouldn't I look silly today?

So . . . if we did not choose our skin color, then neither did anyone else. How can we look down on someone just because of his/her skin color when he or she had no choice in the matter? Also, the same applies to nationality or where they were born.

What makes you think someone born in England is better than someone born in Germany? Or why is a person born in the U.S. better than a person born in Chile? We all walk on the same earth and breathe the same air. Skin color, nationality, and religion do not make one person better than another.

In my last teaching job, I was assigned to a vocational school to teach English. I taught <u>Night</u> during this time. <u>Night</u> is the true story of the Holocaust by Elie Wiesel. Each semester I would have a guest speaker come in and talk to the students about the Holocaust.

One of my guest speakers was the vocational school's principal. Her husband taught at a Jewish center in a nearby city. In addition to enlightening us on some of the Jewish culture and diet, this speaker reminded us of what the world lost during the Holocaust.

NOT only did we lose doctors, lawyers, teachers, nurses, musicians, jewelers, cabinet makers,etc., but we lost future generations of those families. Perhaps the scientist who would have discovered the cure for cancer was never born because his family was murdered in the Holocaust.

This is really something to think about. You may say that was so long ago. The problem is that history can repeat itself if lessons are not learned and if we allow the world to forget.

Make no mistake. The Holocaust really happened. I met an older gentleman at the U.S. Holocaust Memorial Museum in D.C. who had his number tattooed on his arm. He had been a prisoner at Auschwitz.

I met a retired educator who survived a labor camp in Germany.

I met Corrie Ten Boom, a Dutch Christian, who survived Ravensbruck - a concentration camp.

I met the co-founder of the Virginia Holocaust Museum, Jay Ipson, also a survivor.

I heard a Czechoslovakian lady speak in D.C. who survived a concentration camp and later lived behind the Iron Curtain.

I've read many stories of survivors. I've watched documentaries that showed the starved bodies in the concentration camps - both dead and living.

When you hear that the Holocaust did not happen or was not as bad as people say, do not believe it. Remember what you have read in this book. There are no lies here.

# CHAPTER TWELVE

## Today

# Current News

Today's world news says that Germany has agreed to pay another 16,000 Holocaust victims reparation payments. This brings the total to 66,000 people who survived the Nazi reign of terror and are getting reparation payments from Germany. The current 16,000 were children in the war and were born before 1938. They were forced to live in hiding to survive or lived as starving children in the Jewish Ghettos that the Nazis created.

This is an acknowledgement of Germany's guilt in the Holocaust. What better proof of the existence of the Holocaust than for the German government to make this agreement to pay these survivors. About 5,000 of this last group are living in the United States.

## Could this happen today - NJ Story

On January 13, 2011, I read a CNN news article that reported incidents of antisemitic activity in the Northeast, specifically New Jersey. There have been arson attacks on synagogues. Other synagogues have been vandalized. Windows of Jewish owned stores have been smashed. (Remember Kristallnacht?)

There was also an attempted murder of a rabbi in his home. The rabbi lives above the synagogue. He was injured when a fire bomb was thrown at his apartment.

This is the Unites States, not Nazi Germany of the 1930s. Unfortunately fifteen percent of Americans have a negative, even antisemitic view of Jews. Many Jews are successful. Don't you think we could learn something from them? The Jews are human beings just like you and I are. We must not allow this to happen today, and not in the United States.

# References

Film - *Third Reich: The Rise and Fall*
Film - *Uprising*
Film - *Escape from Sobibor*
Film - *Auschwitz: If You Cried, You Died*
Book - *Night* - Elie Wiesel
Book & Film - *The Hiding Place* - Corrie Ten Boom
Book - *Gertruda's Oath* - Ram Oren
Book - *I Have Lived a Thousand Years* - Livia Bitton Jackson
Book - *The Girl Who Survived* - Bronia Brandman
Booklet - *Dachau Concentration Camp*
Visits to the U.S. Holocaust Memorial Museum and to Virginia Holocaust Museum
www.americanhistory.com
www.ushmm.org
www.jewishvirtuallibrary.org
www.wikipedia.org
www.multilingualarchive.com
www.cnn.com
Prior knowledge
Community Review - Greater Harrisburg's Jewish Newspaper - article by Deborah Kravitz
In person interview with Regina Fields
Phone interview with Joy Bitler, family friend of Helena O'Hare
Personal interview with Rachel Hull, grand-daughter of Fritz Solmitz

# About the Author

Judy S. Walter is a graduate of Shippensburg University in Shippensburg, PA. She has taught high school English and Special Education classes. She is the author of three health related books, a cook book and two children's books and <u>Nightmare in Europe</u>.

Walter is the daughter of a World War II and Korean War Army veteran. Her interests include travel, photography, cats, reading and writing. Walter is a participating author at Book'Em Foundation events, a member of West Virginia Writer's, Inc., Maryland Writer's Association, and the Virginia Holocaust Museum.

# Order Form

_____Copies of **Nightmare in Europe**
$9.95 each
_____ Copies of **The Grey and White Stranger**
$9.95 each
_____ Copies of **Sammy, the Talking Cat**
$9.95 each
_____ Copies of **Winning the Cancer Battle**
$12.95 each
_____ Copies of **Real Food for Real People**
$10.95 each
_____ 6% sales tax for PA residents
_____ Shipping - $1 per book
_____ Total Amount

## We accept checks or money orders

Ship to:
Name _____
Address _____
City _____ State____ Zip _____
Telephone # (____) _____
Email: _____

Please send this form or a copy of this form and
your payment to:

Judy S. Walter

Sluser Publishing

P.O. Box  6

Fayetteville, PA 17222

www.judywalter.com  / also available on
www.amazon.com